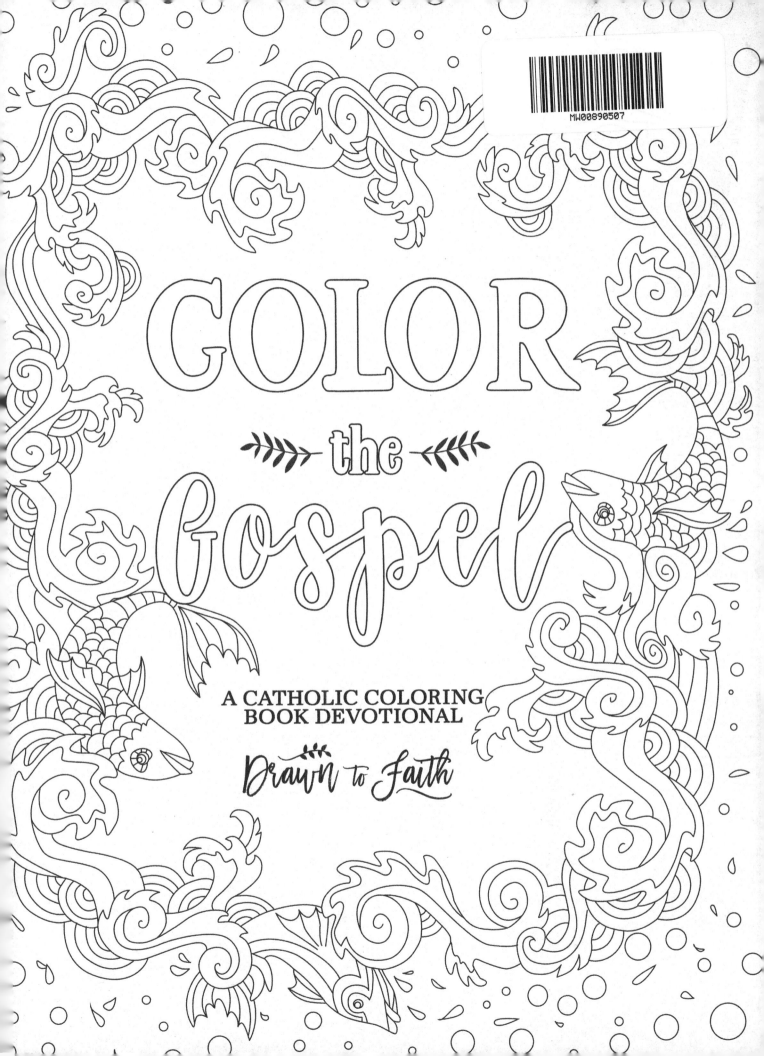

COLOR

≫≫ the ≪≪

Gospel

A CATHOLIC COLORING BOOK DEVOTIONAL

Drawn to Faith

Free Download

www.drawntofaith.com/gospel

YOUR DOWNLOAD CODE: GSP3739

For God so loved the world that he gave his only-begotten Son, so that all who believe in him may not perish, but may have eternal life. For God did not send his Son into the world, in order to judge the world, but in order that the world may be saved through him. Whoever believes in him is not judged. But whoever does not believe is already judged, because he does not believe in the name of the only-begotten Son of God.

John 3:16-18 (CPDV)

Therefore, Jesus said to those Jews who believed in him: "If you will abide in my word, you will truly be my disciples. And you shall know the truth, and the truth shall set you free."

John 8:31-32 (CPDV)

Ask, and it shall be given to you. Seek, and you shall find. Knock, and it shall be opened to you. For everyone who asks, receives; and whoever seeks, finds; and to anyone who knocks, it will be opened.

Matthew 7:7-8 (CPDV)

"This is how you are to pray: Our Father in heaven, hallowed be your name, your kingdom come, your will be done, on earth as in heaven. Give us today our daily bread; and forgive us our debts, as we forgive our debtors; and do not subject us to the final test, but deliver us from the evil one.

Matthew 6:9-13 (NABRE)

If you love me, keep my commandments. And I will ask the Father, and he will give another Advocate to you, so that he may abide with you for eternity: the Spirit of Truth, whom the world is not able to accept, because it neither perceives him nor knows him. But you shall know him. For he will remain with you, and he will be in you.

John 14:15-17 (CPDV)

On the next day, John saw Jesus
coming toward him, and so he said:
"Behold, the Lamb of God. Behold, he
who takes away the sin of the world.
This is the one about whom I said,
'After me arrives a man, who has
been placed ahead of me, because
he existed before me.' And I did not
know him. Yet it is for this reason that
I come baptizing with water: so that
he may be made manifest in Israel."

John 1:29-31 (CPDV)

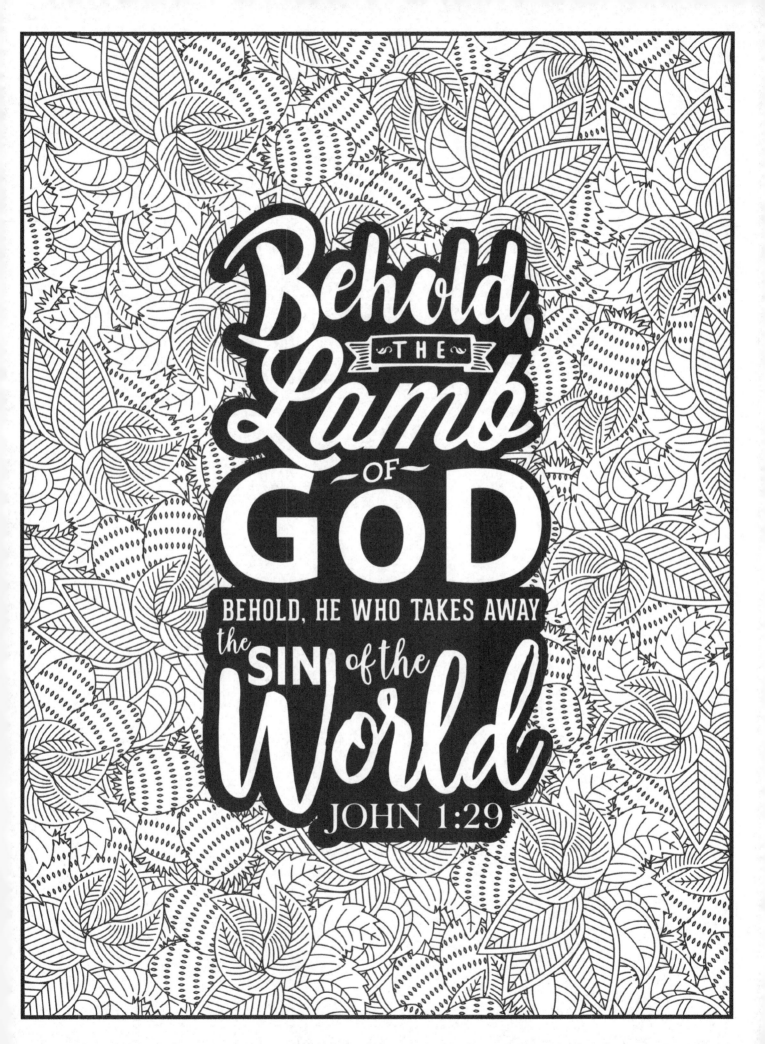

Behold, THE Lamb OF GOD

BEHOLD, HE WHO TAKES AWAY the SIN of the World

JOHN 1:29

"And I say to you, that you are Peter, and upon this rock I will build my Church, and the gates of Hell shall not prevail against it. And I will give you the keys of the kingdom of heaven. And whatever you shall bind on earth shall be bound, even in heaven. And whatever you shall release on earth shall be released, even in heaven."

Matthew 16:18-19 (CPDV)

upon this
ROCK
I WILL BUILD MY
CHURCH
MATTHEW 16:18

Not all who say to me, 'Lord, Lord,' will enter into the kingdom of heaven. But whoever does the will of my Father, who is in heaven, the same shall enter into the kingdom of heaven. Many will say to me in that day, 'Lord, Lord, did we not prophesy in your name, and cast out demons in your name, and perform many powerful deeds in your name?' And then will I disclose to them: 'I have never known you. Depart from me, you workers of iniquity.'

Matthew 7:21-23 (CPDV)

Then, after John was handed over, Jesus went into Galilee, preaching the Gospel of the kingdom of God, and saying: "For the time has been fulfilled and the kingdom of God has drawn near. Repent and believe in the Gospel." And passing by the shore of the Sea of Galilee, he saw Simon and his brother Andrew, casting nets into the sea, for they were fishermen.

Mark 1:14-16 (CPDV)

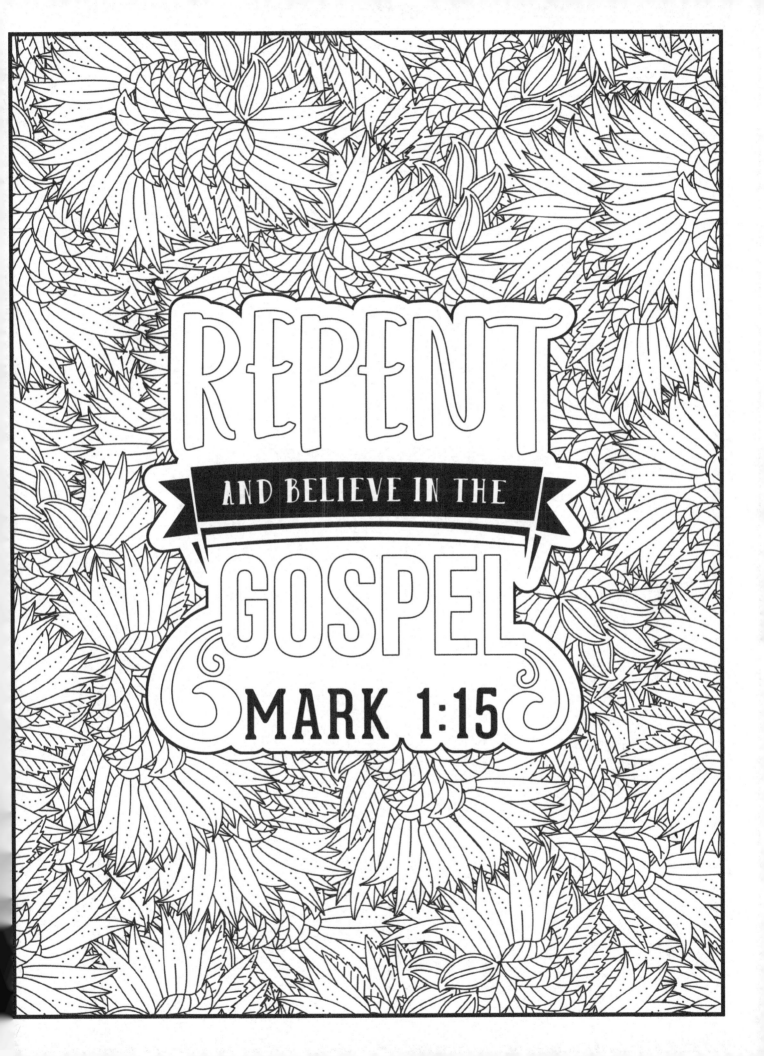

"Come to me, all you who labor and are burdened, and I will give you rest. Take my yoke upon you and learn from me, for I am meek and humble of heart; and you will find rest for yourselves. For my yoke is easy, and my burden light."

Matthew 11:28-30 (NABRE)

In the beginning was the Word, and the Word was with God, and God was the Word. He was with God in the beginning. All things were made through Him, and nothing that was made was made without Him. Life was in Him, and Life was the light of men. And the light shines in the darkness, and the darkness did not comprehend it.

John 1:1-5 (CPDV)

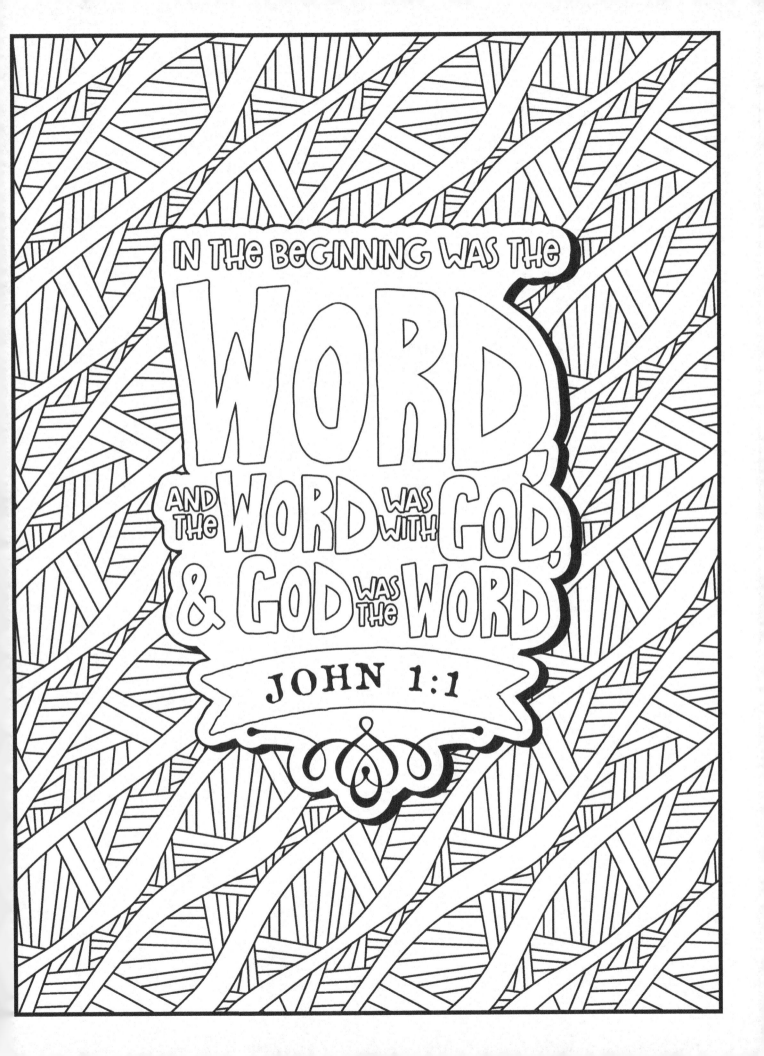

And they brought him. And when he had seen him, immediately the spirit disturbed him. And having been thrown to the ground, he rolled around foaming. And he questioned his father, "How long has this been happening to him?" But he said: "From infancy. And often it casts him into fire or into water, in order to destroy him. But if you are able to do anything, help us and take pity on us." But Jesus said to him, "If you are able to believe: all things are possible to one who believes." And immediately the father of the boy, crying out with tears, said: "I do believe, Lord. Help my unbelief."

Mark 9:19-23 (CPDV)

Then Mary said to the Angel, "How shall this be done, since I do not know man?" And in response, the Angel said to her: "The Holy Spirit will pass over you, and the power of the Most High will overshadow you. And because of this also, the Holy One who will be born of you shall be called the Son of God. And behold, your cousin Elizabeth has herself also conceived a son, in her old age. And this is the sixth month for her who is called barren."

Luke 1:34-36 (CPDV)

And the Word became flesh, and he lived among us, and we saw his glory, glory like that of an only-begotten Son from the Father, full of grace and truth.

John 1:14 (CPDV)

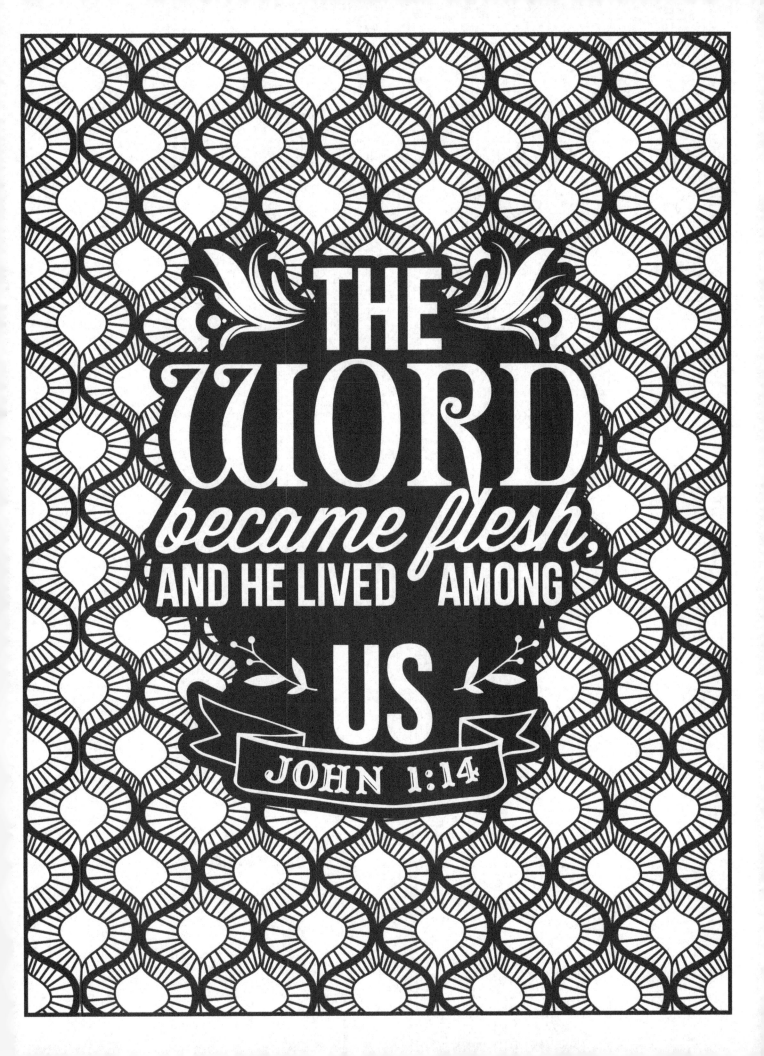

THE WORD became flesh, AND HE LIVED AMONG US

JOHN 1:14

A man named John was sent from God. He came for testimony, to testify to the light, so that all might believe through him. He was not the light, but came to testify to the light. The true light, which enlightens everyone, was coming into the world.

John 1:6-9 (NABRE)

Behold, I am sending you like sheep in the midst of wolves. Therefore, be as prudent as serpents and as simple as doves. But beware of men. For they will hand you over to councils, and they will scourge you in their synagogues. And you shall be led before both rulers and kings for my sake, as a testimony to them and to the Gentiles. But when they hand you over, do not choose to think about how or what to speak. For what to speak shall be given to you in that hour. For it is not you who will be speaking, but the Spirit of your Father, who will speak in you.

Matthew 10:16-20 (CPDV)

Whoever believes and is baptized will be saved; whoever does not believe will be condemned. These signs will accompany those who believe: in my name they will drive out demons, they will speak new languages. They will pick up serpents [with their hands], and if they drink any deadly thing, it will not harm them. They will lay hands on the sick, and they will recover."

Mark 16:16-18 (NABRE)

Finally, he appeared to the eleven, as they sat at table. And he rebuked them for their incredulity and hardness of heart, because they did not believe those who had seen that he had risen again. And he said to them: "Go forth to the whole world and preach the Gospel to every creature."

Mark 16:14-15 (CPDV)

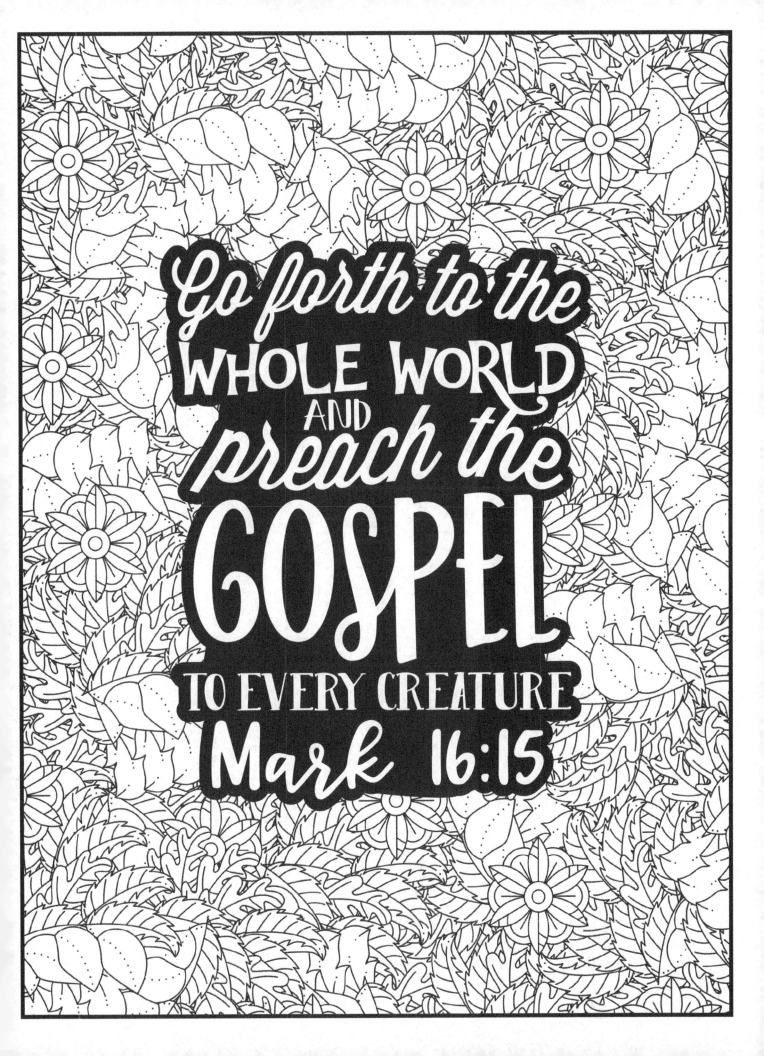

And people were bringing children
to him that he might touch them,
but the disciples rebuked them.
When Jesus saw this he became
indignant and said to them, "Let the
children come to me; do not prevent
them, for the kingdom of God belongs
to such as these. Amen, I say to you,
whoever does not accept the kingdom
of God like a child will not enter it."

Mark 10:13-15 (NABRE)

Whoever DOES NOT ACCEPT THE KINGDOM of God like a child will not ENTER it

MARK 10:15

Then the devil took him to the holy city, and made him stand on the parapet of the temple, and said to him, "If you are the Son of God, throw yourself down. For it is written: 'He will command his angels concerning you' and 'with their hands they will support you, lest you dash your foot against a stone.'" Jesus answered him, "Again it is written, 'You shall not put the Lord, your God, to the test.'"

Matthew 4:5-7 (NABRE)

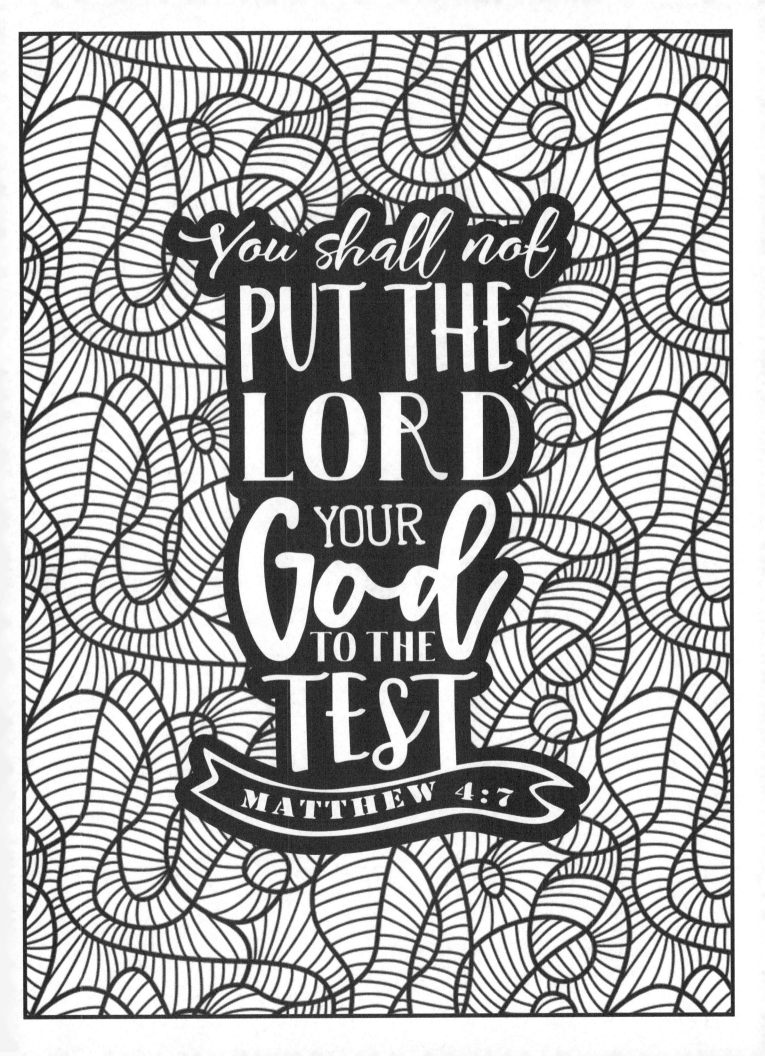

I give you a new commandment:
Love one another. Just as I have
loved you, so also must you love
one another.

John 13:34 (CPDV)

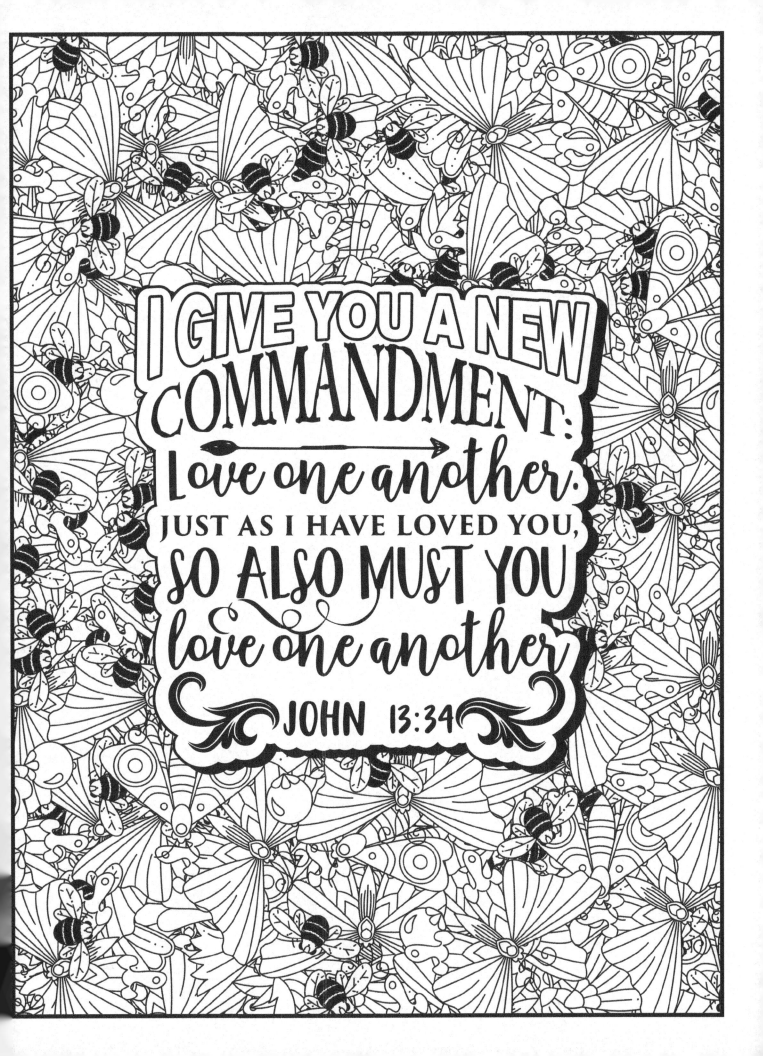

And raising his eyes toward his disciples he said: "Blessed are you who are poor, for the kingdom of God is yours. Blessed are you who are now hungry, for you will be satisfied. Blessed are you who are now weeping, for you will laugh. Blessed are you when people hate you, and when they exclude and insult you, and denounce your name as evil on account of the Son of Man. Rejoice and leap for joy on that day! Behold, your reward will be great in heaven. For their ancestors treated the prophets in the same way.

Luke 6:20-23 (NABRE)

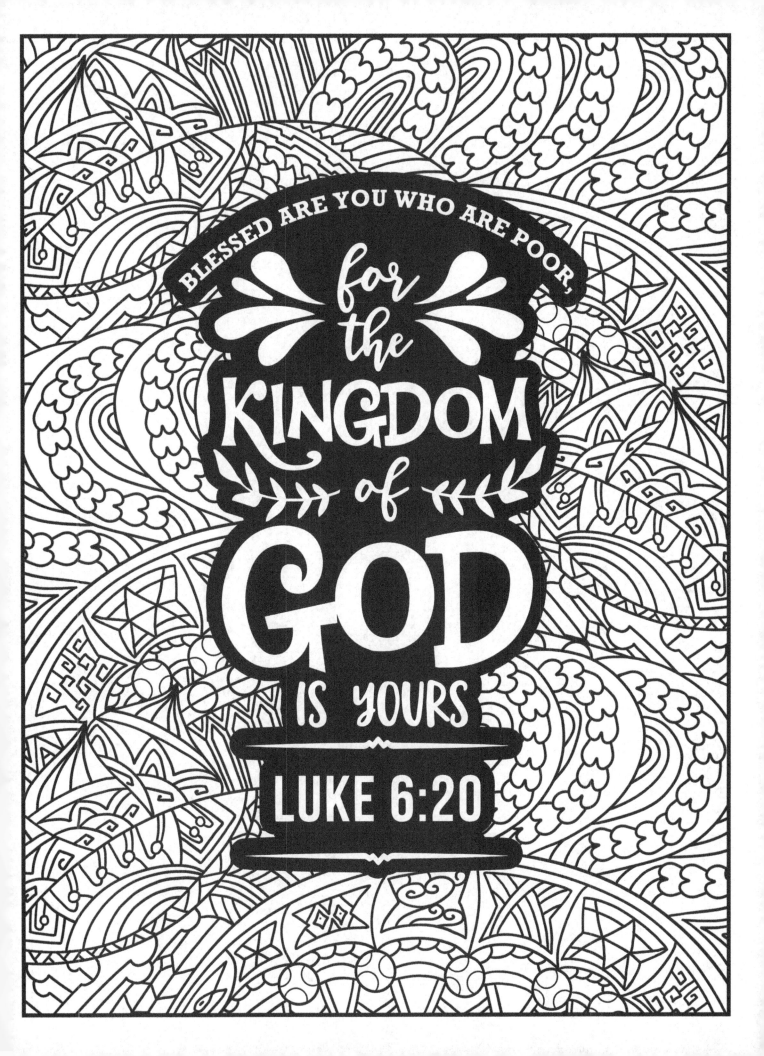

And in response, Jesus said to them:
"Have the faith of God. Amen I say to you,
that whoever will say to this mountain,
'Be taken up and cast into the sea,' and
who will not have hesitated in his heart,
but will have believed: then whatever he
has said be done, it shall be done for him.
For this reason, I say to you, all things
whatsoever that you ask for when praying:
believe that you will receive them, and they
will happen for you. And when you stand to
pray, if you hold anything against anyone,
forgive them, so that your Father, who is in
heaven, may also forgive you your sins.

Mark 11:22-25 (CPDV)

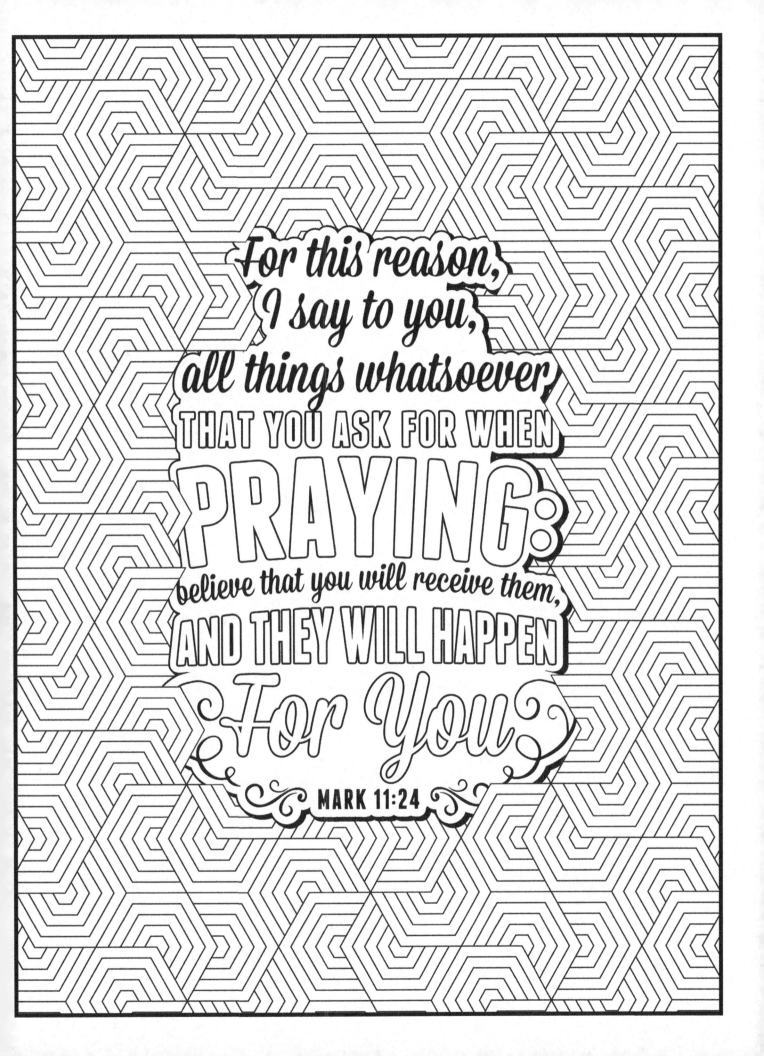

For this reason,
I say to you,
all things whatsoever,
THAT YOU ASK FOR WHEN
PRAYING;
believe that you will receive them,
AND THEY WILL HAPPEN
For You

MARK 11:24

Now tax collectors and sinners were drawing near to him, so that they might listen to him. And the Pharisees and the scribes murmured, saying, "This one accepts sinners and eats with them."

Luke 15:1-2 (CPDV)

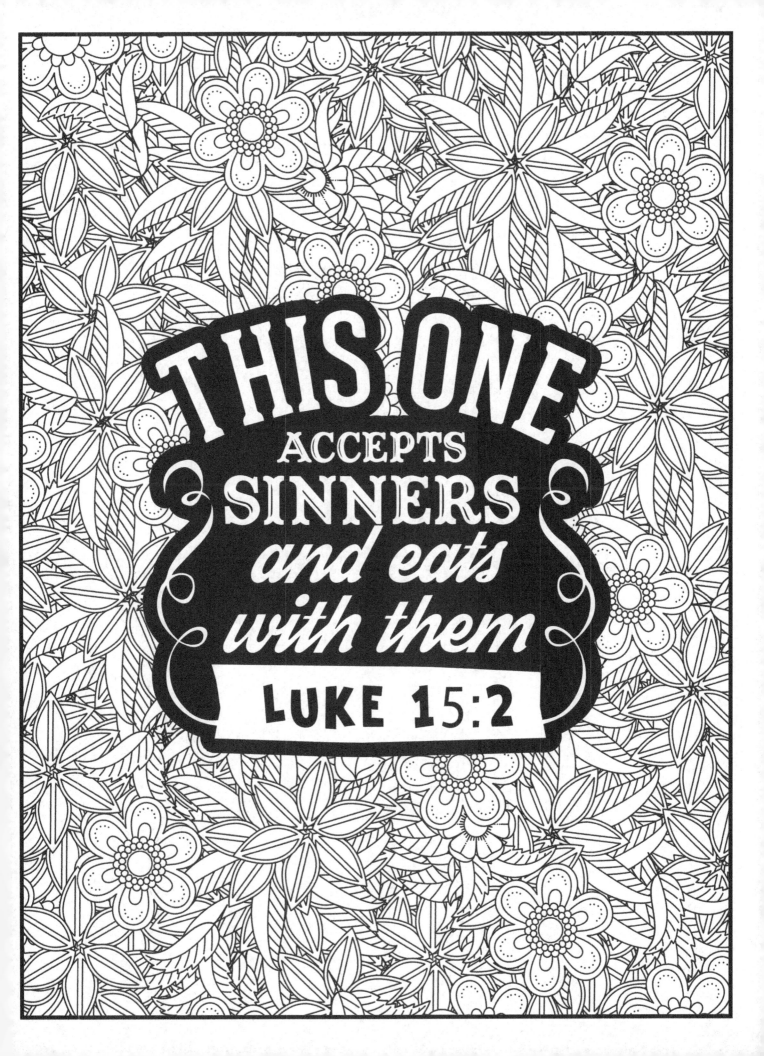

THIS ONE ACCEPTS SINNERS and eats with them
LUKE 15:2

Then he took the bread, said the blessing, broke it, and gave it to them, saying, "This is my body, which will be given for you; do this in memory of me." And likewise the cup after they had eaten, saying, "This cup is the new covenant in my blood, which will be shed for you.

Luke 22:19-20 (NABRE)

THIS IS MY BODY,
WHICH WILL BE GIVEN
FOR YOU.
DO THIS IN
MEMORY OF ME
Luke 22:19

And Jesus answered him: "For the first commandment of all is this: 'Listen, O Israel. The Lord your God is one God. And you shall love the Lord your God from your whole heart, and from your whole soul, and from your whole mind, and from your whole strength. This is the first commandment.' But the second is similar to it: 'You shall love your neighbor as yourself.' There is no other commandment greater than these."

Mark 12:29-31 (CPDV)

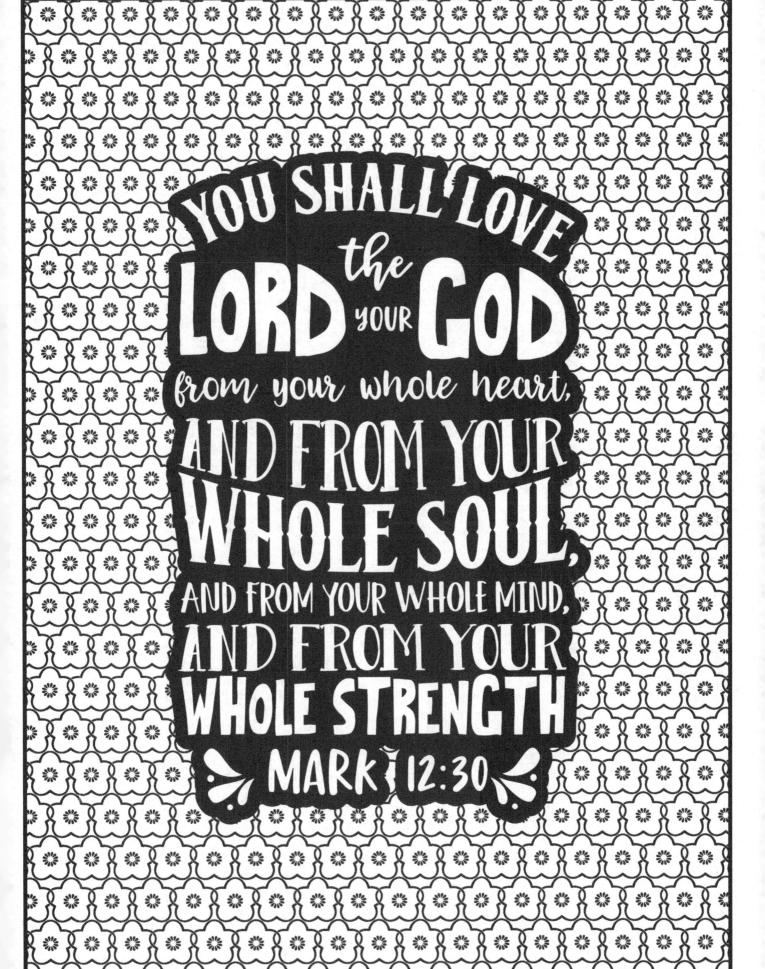

When the ten heard this, they became indignant at James and John. Jesus summoned them and said to them, "You know that those who are recognized as rulers over the Gentiles lord it over them, and their great ones make their authority over them felt. But it shall not be so among you. Rather, whoever wishes to be great among you will be your servant; whoever wishes to be first among you will be the slave of all. For the Son of Man did not come to be served but to serve and to give his life as a ransom for many."

Mark 10:41-45 (NABRE)

The true light, which enlightens everyone, was coming into the world. He was in the world, and the world came to be through him, but the world did not know him.

John 1:9-10 (NABRE)

the TRUE LIGHT which enlightens EVERYONE was COMING into the WORLD

JOHN 1:9

Therefore, do not choose to be anxious, saying: 'What shall we eat, and what shall we drink, and with what shall we be clothed?' For the Gentiles seek all these things. Yet your Father knows that you need all these things. Therefore, seek first the kingdom of God and his justice, and all these things shall be added to you as well.

Matthew 6:31-33 (CPDV)

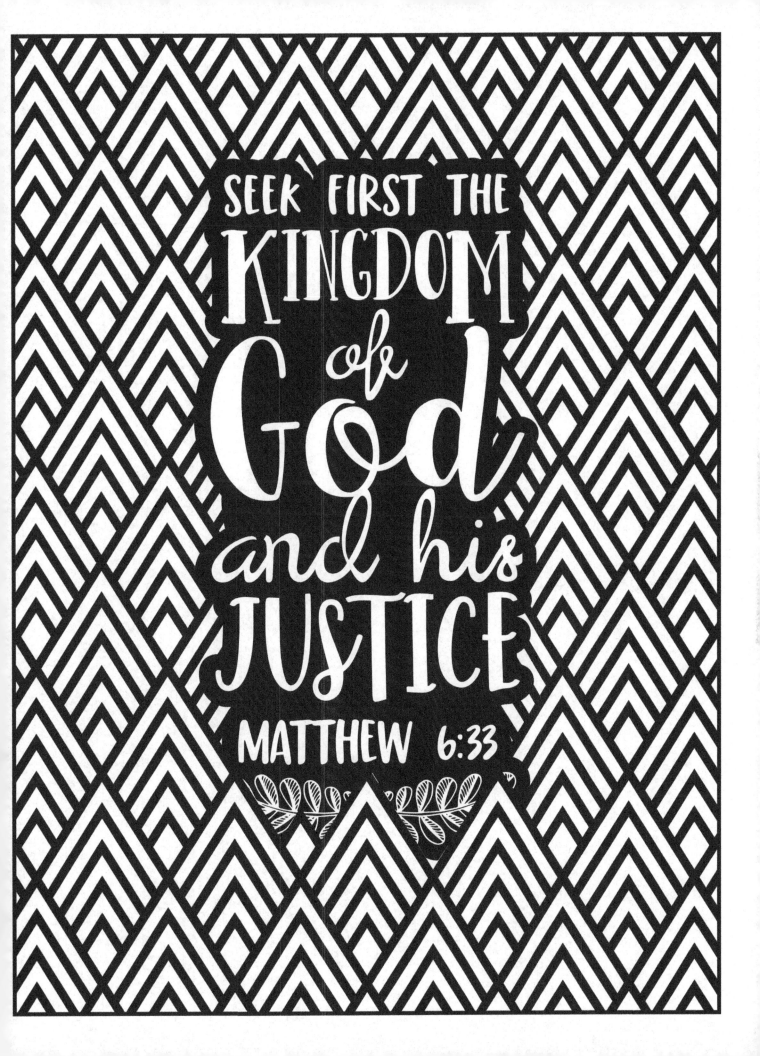

"Do not let your heart be troubled. You believe in God. Believe in me also. In my Father's house, there are many dwelling places. If there were not, I would have told you. For I go to prepare a place for you. And if I go and prepare a place for you, I will return again, and then I will take you to myself, so that where I am, you also may be. And you know where I am going. And you know the way."

John 14:1-4 (CPDV)

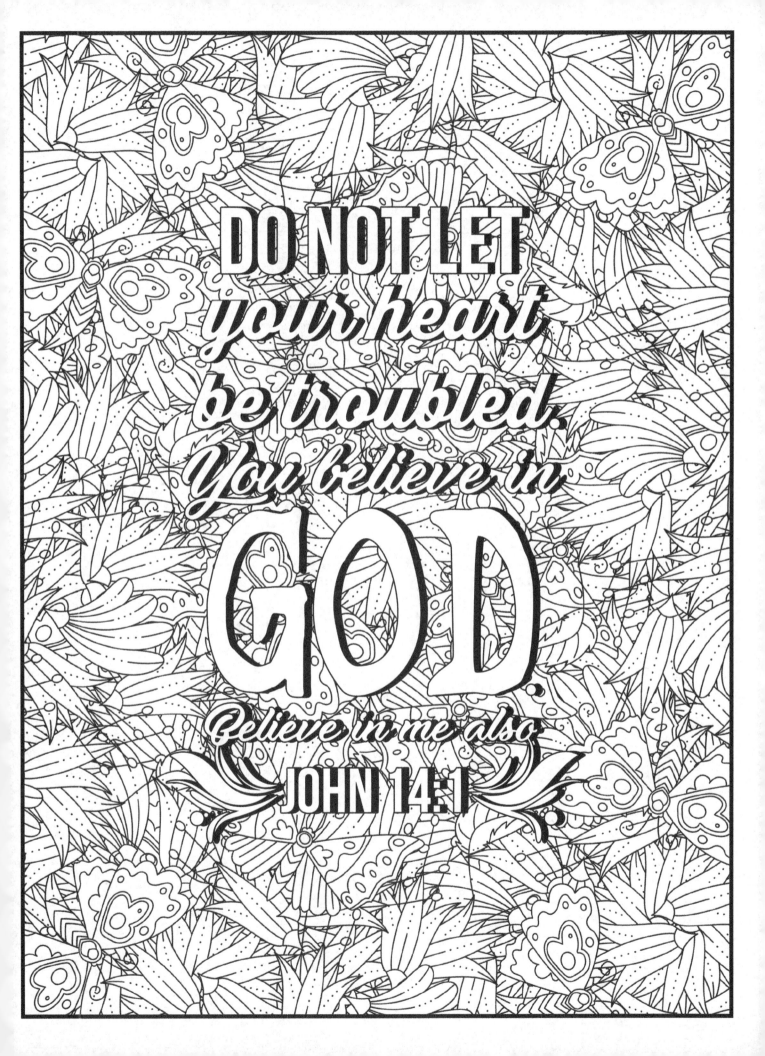

DO NOT LET your heart be troubled. You believe in GOD. Believe in me also

JOHN 14:1

And he said to them: "For so it is written, and so it was necessary, for the Christ to suffer and to rise up from the dead on the third day, and, in his name, for repentance and the remission of sins to be preached, among all the nations, beginning at Jerusalem. And you are witnesses of these things.

Luke 24:46-48 (CPDV)

FOR SO IT IS WRITTEN, AND SO IT WAS NECESSARY, for the Christ TO SUFFER AND TO RISE UP FROM THE DEAD ON THE third day LUKE 24:46

Jesus responded and said to him, "Amen, amen, I say to you, unless one has been reborn anew, he is not able to see the kingdom of God." Nicodemus said to him: "How could a man be born when he is old? Surely, he cannot enter a second time into his mother's womb to be reborn?" Jesus responded: "Amen, amen, I say to you, unless one has been reborn by water and the Holy Spirit, he is not able to enter into the kingdom of God. What is born of the flesh is flesh, and what is born of the Spirit is spirit.

John 3:3-6 (CPDV)

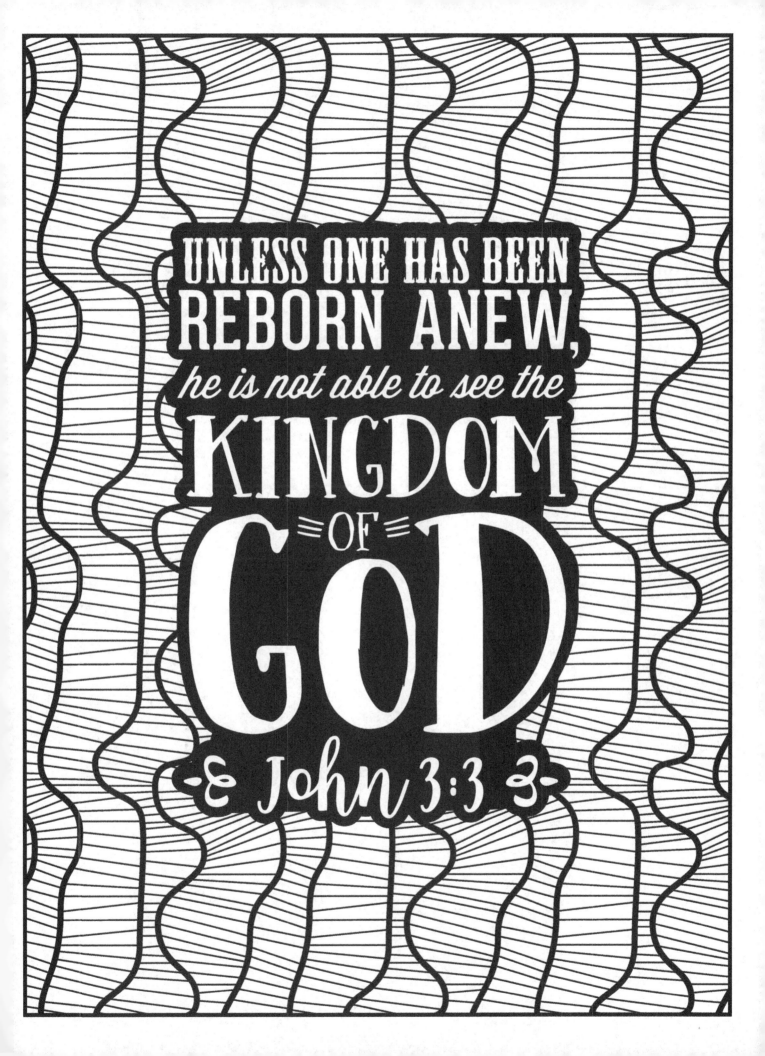

He summoned the crowd with his disciples and said to them, "Whoever wishes to come after me must deny himself, take up his cross, and follow me. For whoever wishes to save his life will lose it, but whoever loses his life for my sake and that of the gospel will save it. What profit is there for one to gain the whole world and forfeit his life? What could one give in exchange for his life?

Mark 8:34-37 (NABRE)

What profit is there FOR ONE TO GAIN the whole WORLD and forfeit his life? MARK 8:36

Do not choose to store up for yourselves treasures on earth: where rust and moth consume, and where thieves break in and steal. Instead, store up for yourselves treasures in heaven: where neither rust nor moth consumes, and where thieves do not break in and steal. For where your treasure is, there also is your heart.

Matthew 6:19-21 (CPDV)

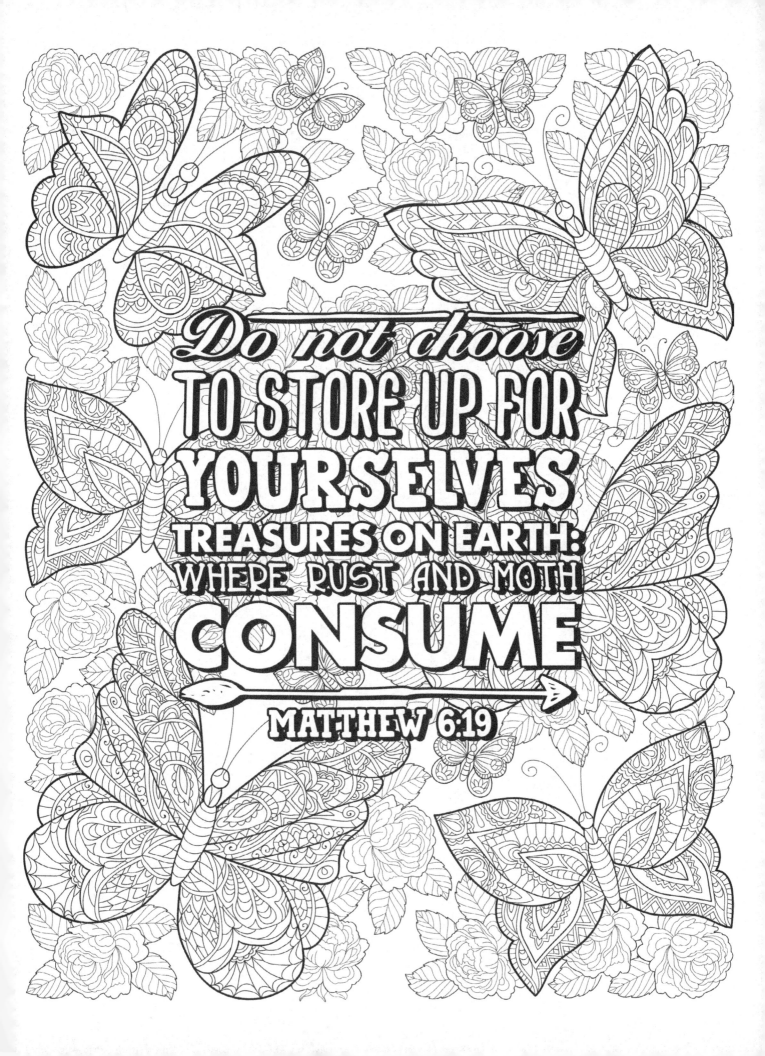

Do not choose TO STORE UP FOR YOURSELVES TREASURES ON EARTH: WHERE RUST AND MOTH CONSUME

MATTHEW 6:19

And he began to teach them that the Son of man must suffer many things, and be rejected by the elders, and by the high priests, and the scribes, and be killed, and after three days rise again. And he spoke the word openly. And Peter, taking him aside, began to correct him. And turning away and looking at his disciples, he admonished Peter, saying, "Get behind me, Satan, for you do not prefer the things that are of God, but the things that are of men."

Mark 8:31-33 (CPDV)

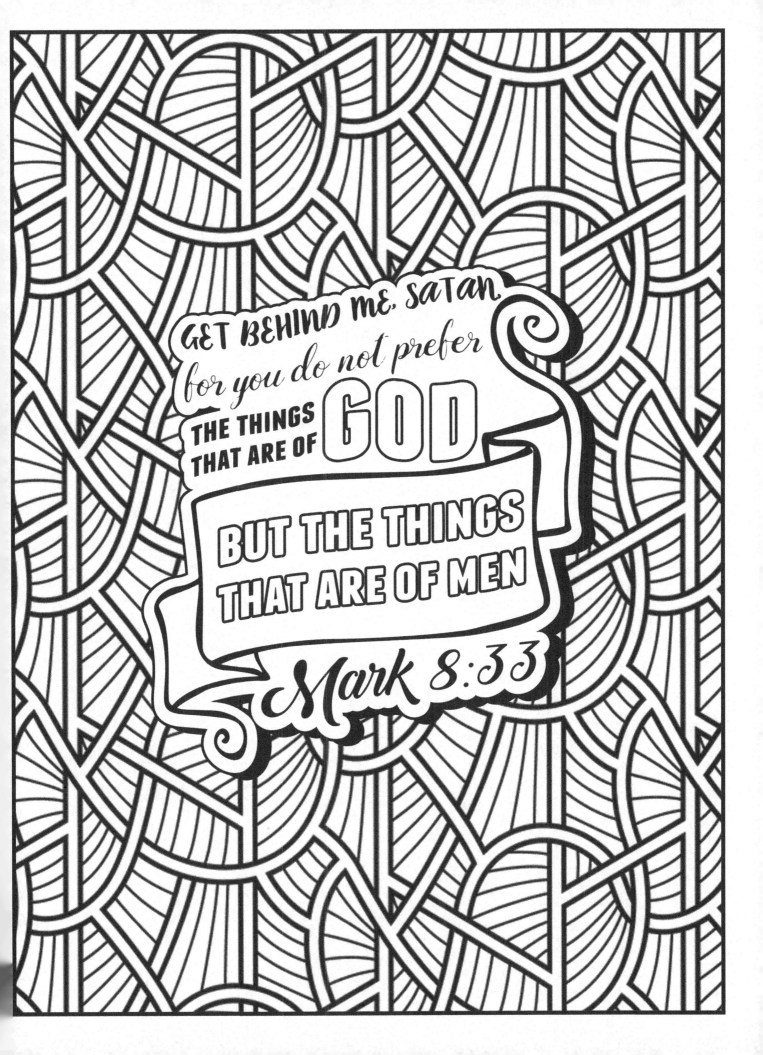

Now they also led out two other criminals with him, in order to execute them. And when they arrived at the place that is called Calvary, they crucified him there, with the robbers, one to the right and the other to the left. Then Jesus said, "Father, forgive them. For they know not what they do." And truly, dividing his garments, they cast lots. And people were standing near, watching. And the leaders among them derided him, saying: "He saved others. Let him save himself, if this one is the Christ, the elect of God."

Luke 23:32-35 (CPDV)

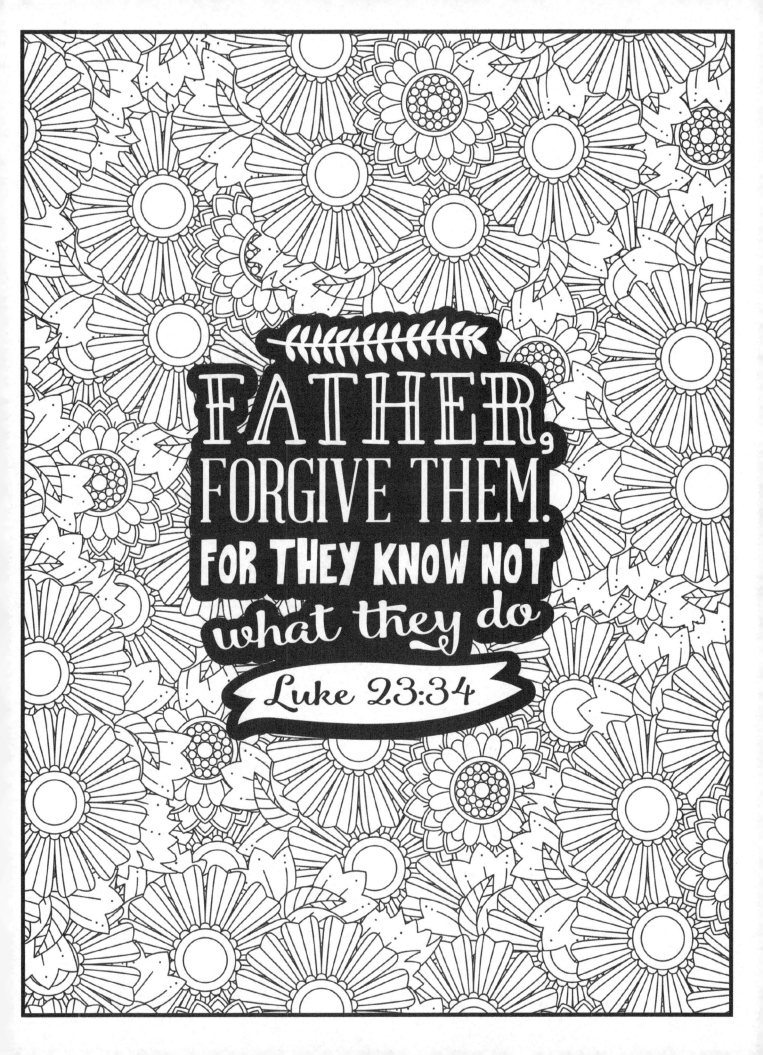

You have heard that it was said:
'An eye for an eye, and a tooth for
a tooth.' But I say to you, do not resist
one who is evil, but if anyone will have
struck you on your right cheek, offer
to him the other also. And anyone
who wishes to contend with you in
judgment, and to take away your
tunic, release to him your cloak also.
And whoever will have compelled you
for one thousand steps, go with him
even for two thousand steps. Whoever
asks of you, give to him. And if anyone
would borrow from you, do not turn
away from him.

Matthew 5:38-42 (CPDV)

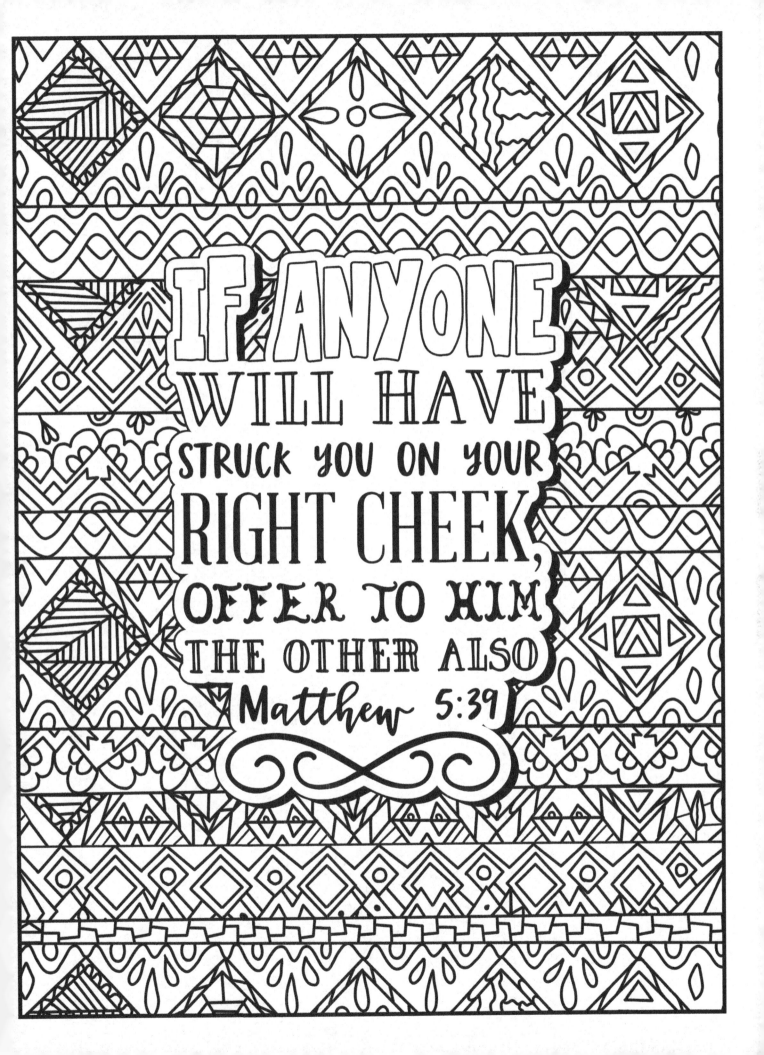

"Do not judge, so that you may not be judged. For with whatever judgment you judge, so shall you be judged; and with whatever measure you measure out, so shall it be measured back to you.

Matthew 7:1-2 (CPDV)

DO NOT judge SO THAT YOU MAY NOT BE JUDGED
MATTHEW 7:1

But I say to you who are listening: Love your enemies. Do good to those who hate you. Bless those who curse you, and pray for those who slander you. And to him who strikes you on the cheek, offer the other also. And from him who takes away your coat, do not withhold even your tunic. But distribute to all who ask of you. And do not ask again of him who takes away what is yours. And exactly as you would want people to treat you, treat them also the same.

Luke 6:27-31 (CPDV)

Then, while they were talking about these things, Jesus stood in their midst, and he said to them: "Peace be with you. It is I. Do not be afraid." Yet truly, they were very disturbed and terrified, supposing that they saw a spirit. And he said to them: "Why are you disturbed, and why do these thoughts rise up in your hearts? See my hands and feet, that it is I myself. Look and touch. For a spirit does not have flesh and bones, as you see that I have."

Luke 24:36-39 (CPDV)

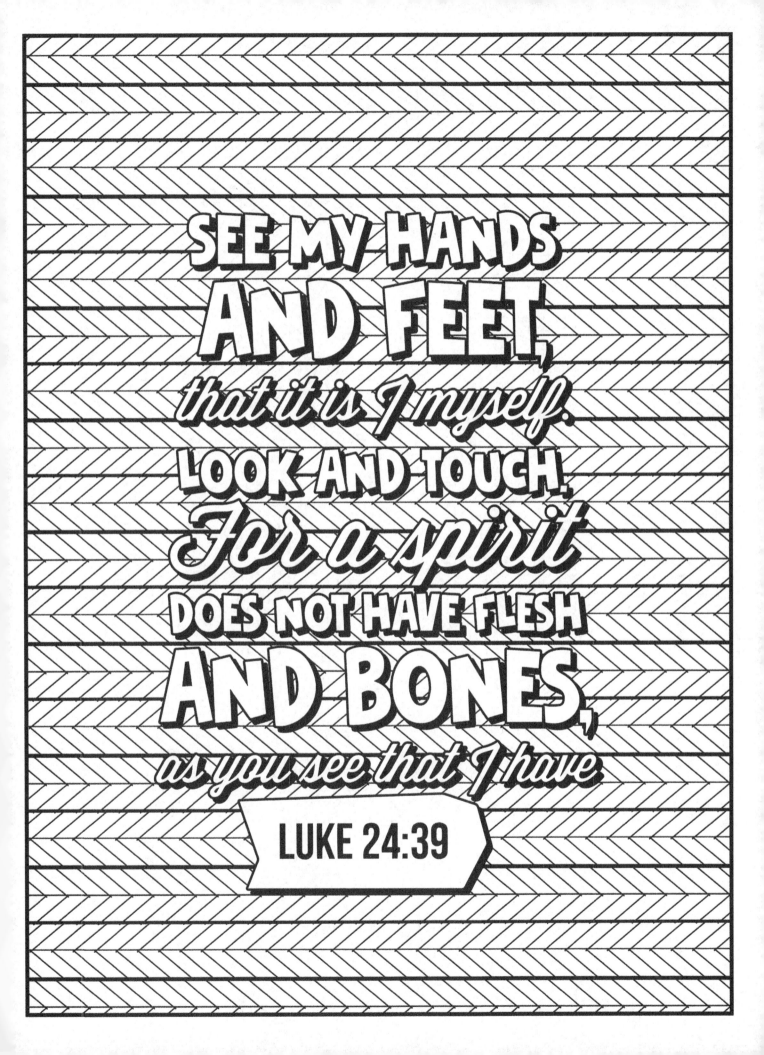

And Jesus, drawing near, spoke to them, saying: "All authority has been given to me in heaven and on earth. Therefore, go forth and teach all nations, baptizing them in the name of the Father and of the Son and of the Holy Spirit, teaching them to observe all that I have ever commanded you. And behold, I am with you always, even to the consummation of the age."

Matthew 28:18-20 (CPDV)

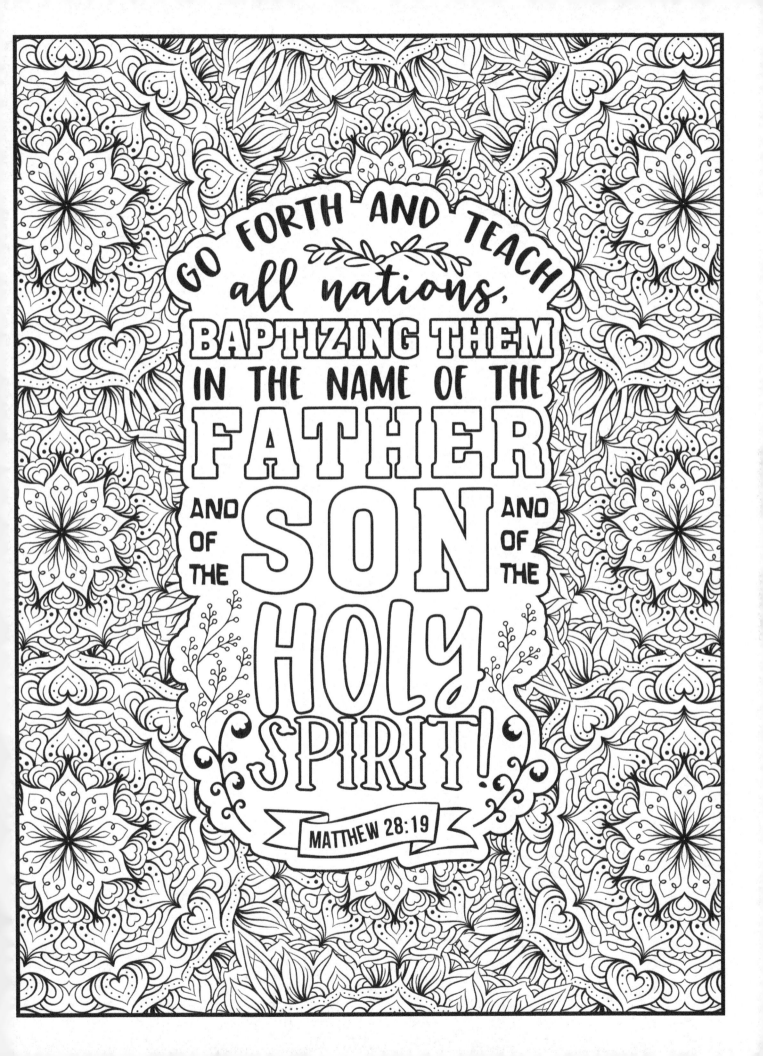

And Jesus, having been baptized, ascended from the water immediately, and behold, the heavens were opened to him. And he saw the Spirit of God descending like a dove, and alighting on him. And behold, there was a voice from heaven, saying: "This is my beloved Son, in whom I am well pleased."

Matthew 3:16-17 (CPDV)

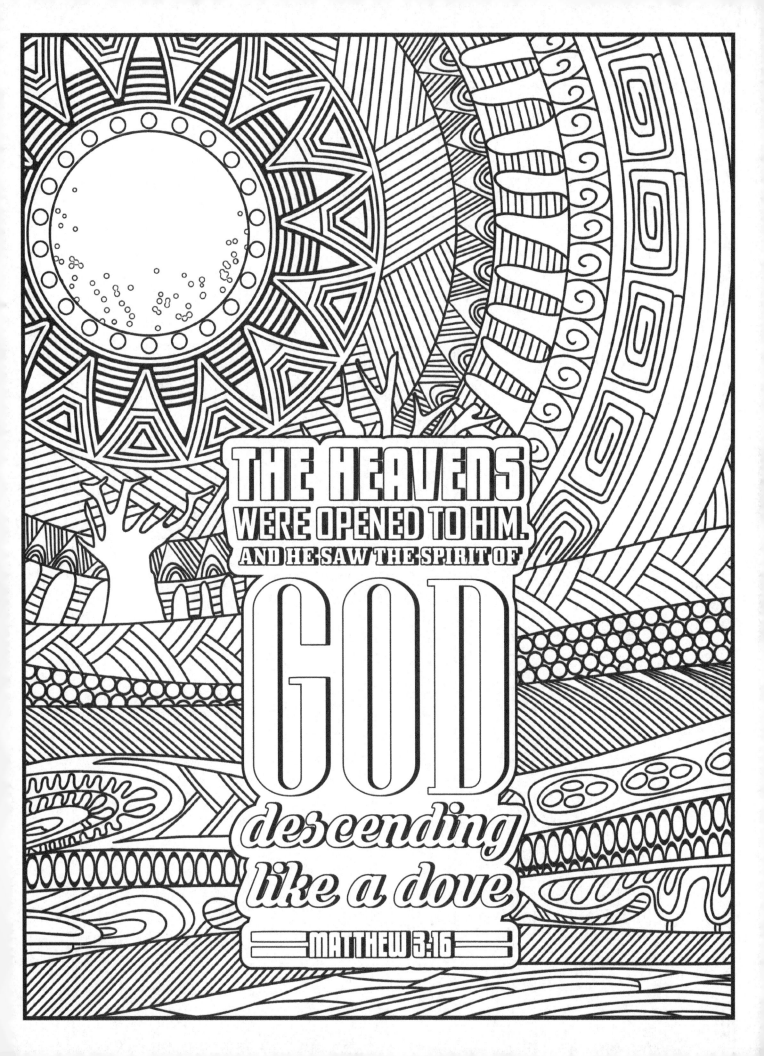

And when the Sabbath had passed, Mary Magdalene, and Mary the mother of James, and Salome bought aromatic spices, so that when they arrived they could anoint Jesus. And very early in the morning, on the first of the Sabbaths, they went to the tomb, the sun having now risen.

Mark 16:1-2 (CPDV)

It was now about noon and darkness
came over the whole land until three
in the afternoon because of an eclipse
of the sun. Then the veil of the temple
was torn down the middle. Jesus cried
out in a loud voice, "Father, into your
hands I commend my spirit"; and when
he had said this he breathed his last.

Luke 23:44-46 (NABRE)

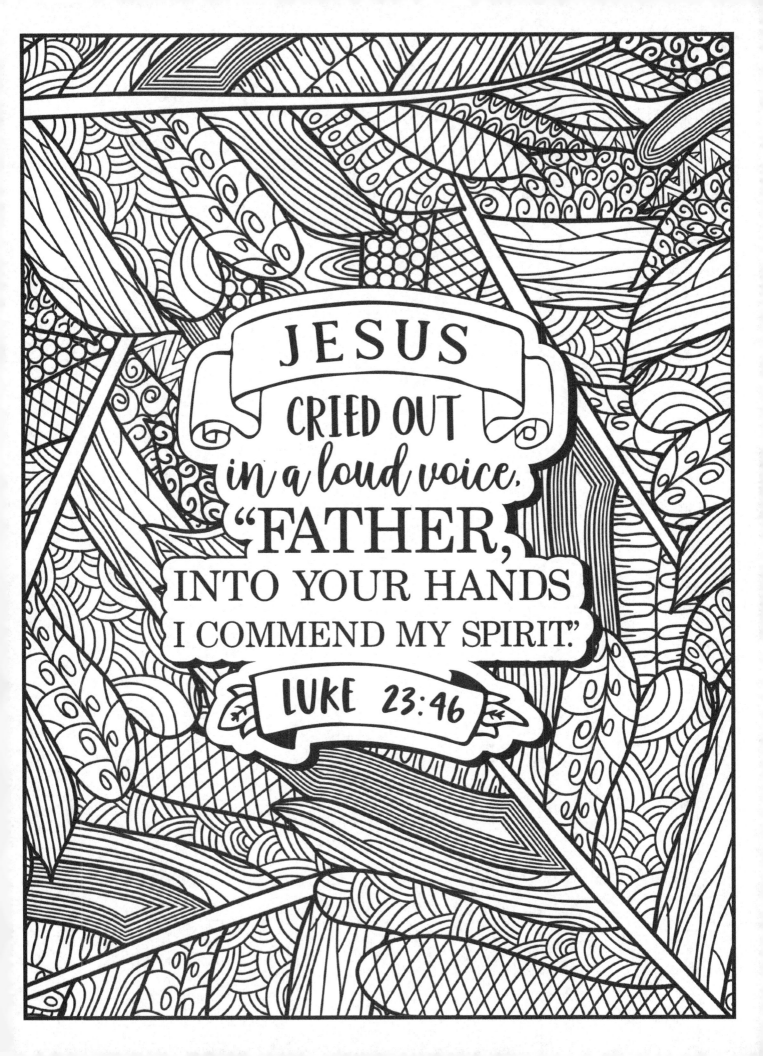

BE SURE TO FOLLOW US ON SOCIAL MEDIA FOR THE LATEST NEWS, SNEAK PEEKS, & GIVEAWAYS

@drawntofaith

Drawn To Faith

@drawntofaith

ADD YOURSELF TO OUR MONTHLY NEWSLETTER FOR FREE DIGITAL DOWNLOADS AND DISCOUNT CODES

www.drawntofaith.com/newsletter

CHECK OUT OUR OTHER BOOKS!

www.drawntofaith.com

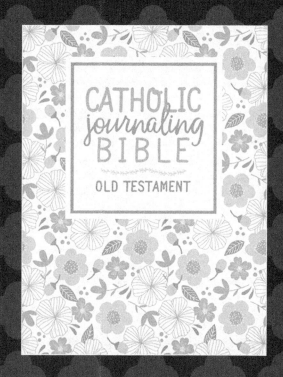
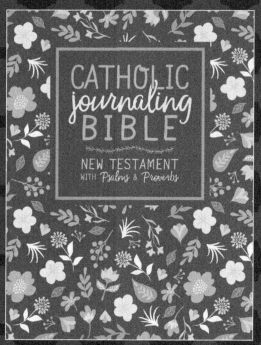
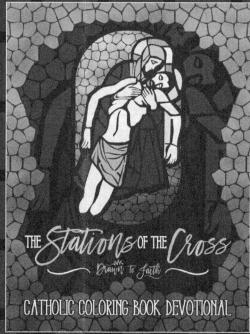
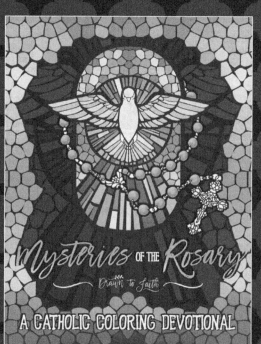

CHECK OUT OUR OTHER BOOKS!

www.drawntofaith.com

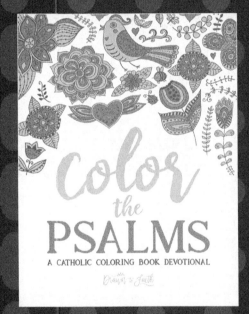

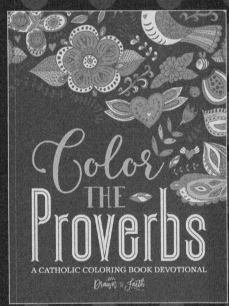

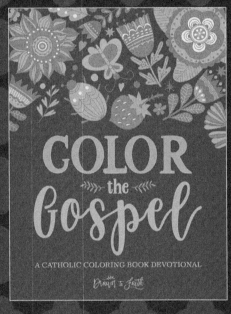

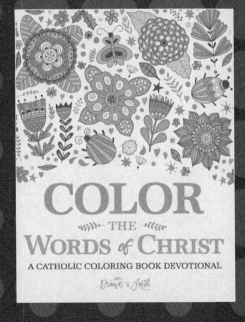

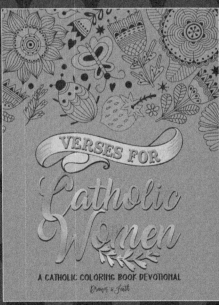

CHECK OUT OUR OTHER BOOKS!

www.drawntofaith.com

Made in the USA
Coppell, TX
31 March 2022

75816718R00057